Dear Readers,

I was recently going through a drawer of old writing from my teenage and college years. I was a constant scribbler: fictions, essays, plays. And poems: finished, unfinished, partly finished. Most were pretty bad, but there were a lot of them. Some had been sent out hopefully to magazines, with a return envelope, duly stamped, in which they were—mostly—returned. These poems had many subjects: peonies, the Hungarian Revolution of 1956, winter, severed heads. The usual.

The poems were written in ink, pencil, ballpoint—whatever came to hand—on various kinds of paper: lined, blank, white, yellow, blue—again, whatever came to hand. Looking at the handwritten originals of the poems in *Dearly*, I see that my methods haven't changed. I use the word 'methods' loosely; I've never had any methods, having never taken any course that might have taught me some. There weren't any such courses in Canada in the late fifties.

Between poetry books, I'd let the handwritten poems accumulate in a drawer. I would work on some, typing them with my four typing fingers, revising them, then retyping them. From time to time I would lay the typed poems out on the floor— much as Jo is shown as doing with her written pages in the film *Little Women*—and then rearrange, add and discard, ponder.

So it has been with the poems in *Dearly*. Handwritten, put in a drawer, typed, revised. These poems were written between 2008 and 2019. During those eleven years, things got darker in the world. Also, I grew older. People very close to me died.

Poetry deals with the core of human existence: life, death, renewal, change; as well as fairness and unfairness, injustice and sometimes justice. The world in all its variety. The weather. Time. Sadness. Joy.

And birds. There are more birds in these poems than there used to be. I wish for even more birds in the next book of poems, should there be one; and I wish also for more birds in the world.

Let us all hope.

Margaret Atwood

# MARGARET ATWOOD

Atwood has won numerous awards including the Arthur C. Clarke Award for Imagination in Service to Society, the Franz Kafka Prize, the Peace Prize of the German Book Trade, the PEN USA Lifetime Achievement Award and the Dayton Literary Peace Prize. In 2019 she was made a member of the Order of the Companions of Honour for services to literature. She has also worked as a cartoonist, illustrator, librettist, scriptwriter, and puppeteer. She lives in Toronto, Canada.

# ALSO BY MARGARET ATWOOD

# DEARLY

## MARGARET ATWOOD

VINTAGE

1 3 5 7 9 10 8 6 4 2

Vintage is part of the Penguin Random House group of companies
whose addresses can be found at global.penguinrandomhouse.com

Penguin
Random House
UK

Copyright © O. W. Toad, Ltd. 2020

O. W. Toad, Ltd. has asserted her right to be identified as the author of this
Work in accordance with the Copyright, Designs and Patents Act 1988

First published in Vintage in 2021
First published in hardback by Chatto & Windus in 2020

penguin.co.uk/vintage

A CIP catalogue record for this book is available from the British Library

ISBN 9781529113280

Printed and bound in Great Britain by Clays Ltd, Elcograf S.p.A.

The authorised representative in the EEA is Penguin Random House Ireland,
Morrison Chambers, 32 Nassau Street, Dublin D02 YH68

Penguin Random House is committed to a sustainable future
for our business, our readers and our planet. This book is made
from Forest Stewardship Council® certified paper.

MIX
Paper from
responsible sources
FSC
www.fsc.org
FSC® C018179

*For Graeme, in absentia*

# CONTENTS

## I.

## II.

## V.

I.

These are the late poems.
Most poems are late
of course: too late,
like a letter sent by a sailor
that arrives after he's drowned.

Too late to be of help, such letters,
and late poems are similar.
They arrive as if through water.

Whatever it was has happened:
the battle, the sunny day, the moonlit
slipping into lust, the farewell kiss. The poem
washes ashore like flotsam.

Or late, as in late for supper:
all the words cold or eaten.
Scoundrel, plight, and vanquished,
or linger, bide, awhile,
forsaken, wept, forlorn.
Love and joy, even: thrice-gnawed songs.
Rusted spells. Worn choruses.

It's late, it's very late;
too late for dancing.
Still, sing what you can.
Turn up the light: sing on,
sing: On.

Cats suffer from dementia too. Did you know that?
Ours did. Not the black one, smart enough
to be neurotic and evade the vet.
The other one, the furrier's muff, the piece of fluff.
She'd writhe around on the sidewalk
for chance pedestrians, whisker
their trousers, though not when she started losing
what might have been her mind. She'd prowl the night
kitchen, taking a bite
from a tomato here, a ripe peach there,
a crumpet, a softening pear.
*Is this what I'm supposed to eat?*
*Guess not. But what? But where?*
Then up the stairs she'd come, moth-footed,
owl-eyed, wailing
like a tiny, fuzzy steam train: *Ar-woo! Ar-woo!*
So witless and erased. *O, who?*
Clawing at the bedroom door
shut tight against her. *Let me in,*
*enclose me, tell me who I was.*
No good. No purring. No contentment. Out
into the darkened cave of the dining room,
then in, then out, forlorn.
And when I go that way, grow fur, start howling,
scratch at your airwaves:
no matter who I claim I am
or how I love you,
turn the key. Bar the window.

Were things good then?
Yes. They were good.
Did you know they were good?
At the time? Your time?

No, because I was worrying
or maybe hungry
or asleep, half of those hours.
Once in a while there was a pear or plum
or a cup with something in it,
or a white curtain, rippling,
or else a hand.
Also the mellow lamplight
in that antique tent,
falling on beauty, fullness,
bodies entwined and cherishing,
then flareup, and then gone.

Mirages, you decide:
everything was never.
Though over your shoulder there it is,
your time laid out like a picnic
in the sun, still glowing,
although it's night.

Don't look behind, they say:
You'll turn to salt.
Why not, though? Why not look?
Isn't it glittery?
Isn't it pretty, back there?

## PASSPORTS

We save them, as we save those curls
culled from our kids' first haircuts, or from lovers
felled too early. Here are

all of mine, safe in a file, their corners
clipped, each page engraved
with trips I barely remember.

Why was I wandering from there to there
to there? God only knows.
And the procession of wraiths' photos

claiming to prove that I was me:
the faces greyish disks, the fisheyes
trapped in the noonhour flashflare

with the sullen jacklit stare
of a woman who's just been arrested.
Sequenced, these pics are like a chart

of moon phases fading to blackout; or
like a mermaid doomed to appear onshore
every five years, and each time altered

to something a little more dead:
skin withering in the parching air,
marooned hair thinning as it dries,
cursed if she smiles or cries.

## BLIZZARD

My mother, sleeping.
Curled up like a spring fern
although she's almost a century.

I speak into her topmost ear,
the one thrust up like a wrinkled stone
above the hills of the pillows:

Hello! Hello!
But she shows a clenched resistance
to waking up.

She's down too deep, a diver
plunged into dangerous caverns:
it's blank in there.

She's dreaming, however.
I can tell by the way she's frowning,
and her strong breathing.

Maybe she's making her way
down one more white river,
or walking across the ice.

There are no more adventures for her
in the upper air, in this room
with her bed and the family pictures.

Let's go out and fight the storm,
she used to say. So maybe
she's fighting it.

Meanwhile I watch a spider
laying a trail across the ceiling,
little dust messenger.

The clock ticks and the day shrivels.
Dusk sifts down on us.
How long should I stay?

I put my hand on her forehead,
stroke her wispy hair.
How tall she used to be,

how we've all dwindled.
It's time for her to go deeper,
into the blizzard ahead of her,

both dark and light, like snow.
Why can't I let go of her?
Why can't I let her go?

# COCONUT

There were more things to buy right after the war.
Oranges made a comeback
and black and white morphed into rainbow.
Not yet avocados,

though suddenly, in the slack tide
of winter, in our cellar,
a coconut materialized
like the round hard hairy breast
of some wooden sasquatch.

Why the cellar?
That's where the axe was.

We drove a long steel nail
into each of the three soft eyes
and drained out the sweetish water.
Then we stood the globe on a block
and hacked it apart.

The pieces clattered over the floor,
which was not clean back then
in the age of coal and cinders.

First taste of sheer ambrosia!
Though mixed with ash and the shards of destruction
as Heaven always is, if you read the texts closely.

We go away, we bring things back
from that alien moon shore
where you can't get the same pills as here,
nor toothpaste, nor local beer.
We'll give these foreign things away,
the ones we bought at stalls:
folkloric knitting, droll hardware,
wooden trolls. Shells, hunks of rock.
They silt up our luggage.
They're souvenirs for our friends,
remembrances.

But who is to remember what?
It's a cute cat hat, but you've never been there.
I can remember buying it
and you can remember that I once
remembered: I remembered
something for you.
It was a sunny day,
though airless. The children had small heads
and pale hair.

I appear in other people's dreams
much oftener than I used to.
Sometimes naked, they say,
or cooking: I seem to cook a lot.
Sometimes as an old dog
carrying a rolled-up letter
in snaggle teeth, addressed to: *Soon.*
Sometimes as a skeleton

in a green satin frock.
I'm always there for a reason,
so the dreamers tell me;
I wouldn't know.

This is what I've brought back for you
from the dreamlife, from the alien moon shore,
from the place with no clocks.
It has no colour, but it has powers,
though I don't know what they are
nor how it unlocks.

Here, it's yours now.
Remember me.

## THE TIN WOODWOMAN GETS A MASSAGE

On the flannel sheet
in the pose of a deadman's float,
face down. The hands descend,
ignore the skin,
the xylophone of spine,
evade the blobs and lobes,
head for deep tissue,

go for the little hinges
that creak like tiny frogs—
twang the catgut strings
of the tight bruised tendons.

How rusted shut I am,
how locked, how oxidized.
Old baked-beans can,
Tin Woodwoman left in the rain.
Movement equals pain.
How corroded.

Who was it used to complain
he didn't have a brain?
Some straw-man cloth boy.

Me, it's the heart:
that's the part lacking.
I used to want one:
a dainty cushion of red silk
dangling from a blood ribbon,
fit for sticking pins in.
But I've changed my mind.
Hearts hurt.

If there were no emptiness, there would be no life.
Think about it.
All those electrons, particles, and whatnot
crammed in next to each other like junk in an attic,
like trash in a compactor
smashed together in a flat block
so there's nothing but plasma:
no you no me.

Therefore I praise vacancy.
Vacant lots with their blowing plastics and teasels,
vacant houses, their furze of dust,
vacant stares, blue as the sky through windows.
Motels with the word *Vacancy*
flashing outside, a neon arrow pointing,

pointing at the path to be taken
to the bored front desk, to the key-shaped key
on the dangling brown leather key holder,

the key that opens the vacant room
with its scored linoleum floor a blear-eyed yellow
its flowery couch and wilted cushions
its swaybacked bed, smelling of bleach and mildew
its stuttering radio
its ashtray that was here
seventy years ago.

That room has been static for me so long:
an emptiness   a void   a silence
containing an unheard story
ready for me to unlock.

Let there be plot.

# II.

# HEALTH CLASS (1953)

Girls, girls, girls, girls, girls!
Simmer down!
This is not a three-ring circus!
This is a classroom.
Today we will talk about Blood.
Silence please!

You think I can't see you from up here?
I know your tricks and slurs,
I know your whispers,
I know where you'd rather be
and your favoured postures,
all your sprawls.

You like to pretend I'm funny
but I frighten you:
I who was once pink gelatin
am now a cold grey moon
waiting in your future.
You'll need me then.

I'll turn my bone face toward you.
I'll give dry light.

## A GENRE PAINTING

Here are the tulips,
budded and full-blown,
their swoops and dips, their gloss and poses,
the satin of their darks.

Here are the linen napkins,
texture and crinkle,
the way they soak up light
from the dwindled candle,
the light blues of their shadows.

Here are the skinned rabbits
hanging from strings
opened to muscle, to shiny gristle,
to raw flesh you can smell:
hot rust, swamp water.

Here is the woman working a knife
among onions and innards,
her sleeves turned back, besmeared.
She's looking at us aslant:
she knows what bodies eat.

This is her job or prayer,
her grace, her offering:
these guts and dying petals,
the candle guttering down.

# PRINCESS CLOTHING

i.

Too many people talk about what she should wear
so she will be fashionable, or at least
so she will not be killed.

Women have moved in next door
wrapped in pieces of cloth
that lack approval.

They're setting a bad example.
Get out the stones.

ii.

Fur is an issue too:
her own and some animal's.
Once the world was nearly stripped of feathers,
all in the cause of headgear.

What was it for, my love,
this ripoff of the birds?
Once there was nothing she wouldn't do
to render herself alluring.
So many items attached to her head:
ribbons and ships, all curling.

Now her torso lies in the ditch
like a lost glove, like a tossed book
mostly unsaid. Unread.
In the high palace of words, one princess the less.

iii.

Oh beware,
uncover your hair
or else they will burn down your castle.
Wait a minute: Cover it!
Hair. So controversial.

iv.

As for feet, they were always a problem.
Toes, heels, and ankles
take turns being obscene.
Little glass slippers, the better to totter.

Many things that are not what you want
arrive in the disguise of flowers.
Lotus foot, the petals
broken bones.

v.

Wool worn next to the skin
was once an army decree.
In mid-battle it's hard to shower.
Wool deterred microbes and did not stink,
or not as much. That was the theory.
Here you go: cashmere!
But armpits: drawbacks, damp as a groin,
even if pink:
not feminine.

vi.

Cotton on the other hand
was crackly. Still is.
Avoid it when making recordings.
You don't want it messing with the ghost voice
of yourself you leave behind in the air.

vii.

Silk, however,
is best for shrouds.
That's where it comes from, silk:
those seven veils the silkworms keep spinning,
hoping they will be butterflies.
Then they get boiled, and then unscrolled.

It's what you hope too, right?
That beyond death, there's flight?
After the shrouding, up you'll rise,
delicate wings and all. Oh honey,
it won't be like that.
Not quite.

# CICADAS

Finally after nine years
of snouting through darkness
he inches up scarred bark
and cuts loose the yammer of desire:

the piercing one-note of a jackhammer,
vibrating like a slow bolt of lightning
splitting the air
and leaving a smell like burnt tarpaper.

*Now* it says *Now* it says *Now*
clinging with six clawed legs
and close by, a she like a withered ear,
a shed leaf, brown and veined,
shivers in sync and moves closer.

This is it, time is short, death is near, but first,
first, first, first
in the hot sun, searing, all day long,
in a month that has no name:
this annoying noise of love. This maddening racket.
This—admit it—song.

## DOUBLE-ENTRY SLUG SEX

If we could reproduce by bud
or spore, there would not be these duels.

Or if each could swivel an identical
organ into the other's ear
while both twirled in the air
suspended from a shimmering rope
of tears and glue, like a tip-top
highwire act,

that would work. It does for slugs:
Look at those pearly eggs!

(More future lacework lettuces.)

Unless they both get stuck.
That too can happen.

No help for it but chewing off
a penis. What then, humans?
If it were yours? Imagine:

The post-deed conversation: apophallation.

*My turn! You bit off mine last time.*

*Get on with it or we'll be here all night,*
*fair game for predators.*

*I don't care! And I don't want to live!*
*You never loved me!*
*You only loved my ear!*

By daylight something's got to give.
Or someone. Some one
has got to give. A given.
That's how we carry on.

# EVERYONE ELSE'S SEX LIFE

Everyone else's sex life seems so impossible.
Surely not, we think:
surely not this into that!
Not such a dirty mouth
and such bad teeth!
Those cooked prunes, those wattles!

Please, keep your clothes on.
They exist for a reason:
to save you from yourself,
your own voyeur.

Nobody looks like a movie star
not even movie stars
on their days off,
rambling along the street
hunting for decent eats
and anonymity, without luck.

Nobody, except to themselves
in their own heads when drunk,
or if they're narcissists, when sober.

Or when in love. Oh yes, *In Love*,
that demented rose-red circus tent
whose half-light forgives all visuals,
fig-leaves our lovers,
and softens our own brains
and the pain of our sawdust pratfalls.

So tempting, that midway faux-marble arch,
both funfair and classical—
so Greek, so Barnum,
such a beacon,
with a sign in gas-blue neon:

*Love! This way!*
*In!*

## BETRAYAL

When you stumble across your lover and your friend
naked in or on your bed
there are things that might be said.

Goodbye is not one of them.
You'll never close that clumsily opened door,
they'll be stuck in that room forever.

But did they have to be so naked?
So minus grace?
Floundering around as if in a spring puddle?

The legs too spindly, the waists too thick,
the flubbers here and there,
the tufts of hair...

Yes, it was a betrayal,
but not of you.
Only of some idea you'd had

of them, soft-lit and mystic,
with snowfall sifting down
and a mauve December sunset—

not this gauche flash,
this flesh akimbo,
caught in the glare of your stare.

# FRIDA KAHLO, SAN MIGUEL, ASH WEDNESDAY

You faded so long ago
but here in the souvenir arcade
you're everywhere:
the printed cotton bags, the pierced tin boxes,
the scarlet T-shirts, the beaded crosses;
your coiled braids, your level stare,
your body of a deer or martyr.

It's a meme you can turn into
if your ending's strange enough
and ardent, and involves much pain.
The rope of a hanged man brings good luck;
saints dangle upside down
or offer their breasts on a plate
and we wear them, we invoke them,
insert them between our flesh and danger.

Fireworks, two streets over.
Something's burning somewhere,
or did burn, once.
A torn silk veil, a yellowing letter:
*I'm dying here.*
Love on a skewer,
a heart in flames.
We breathe you in, thin smoke,
grief in the form of ashes.

Yesterday the children smashed
their hollowed eggs on the heads of others,
baptizing them with glitter.

Shell fragments litter the park
like the wings of crushed butterflies,
like sand, like confetti:
azure, sunset, blood,
your colours.

What if I didn't want all that—
what he prophesied I could do
while coming to no good
and making my name forever?
Dye my hair black, pierce my face,
spew out fuckshaped energy,
hook up, kick back.
Wallow in besmirching fame.

What if I said No Thank You
to Mr. Musician God,
to sex for favours?
What if I stayed right here?
Right in my narrowing hometown
(which will later be burned down)
thinking of others first
and being manless and pitiable?
I'd have a dark-blue leather purse,
and crochet cotton gifts
—dolls' hats, toilet-roll covers—
the nieces would throw out later.
Then I could cry about failure,
pale, sere, minor.

At least I would not be brazen,
like a shield maiden, like a fender.
At least I would not be brash
and last seen alive
that day in mid-November
at the gas station, shivering, hitching,
in the dusk, just before

SHADOW


Someone wants your body.

What's the deal?
Beg, borrow, buy, or steal?
Gutter or pedestal?
That's how it is with bodies
that someone wants.

What's it worth to you?
A rose, a diamond,
a cool million, a joke, a drink?
The fiction that this one likes you?

You could bestow it, this body,
like the generous creature you are,
or blackout and have it snatched
and you'd never know.

Kiss it goodbye, the body
that was once yours.
It's off and running,
it's rolled in furs, it's dancing
or bleeding out in a meadow.

You didn't need it anyway,
it attracted too much attention.
Better with only a shadow.

Someone wants your shadow.

# SONGS FOR MURDERED SISTERS

*A cycle for baritone*

### I. EMPTY CHAIR

Who was my sister
Is now an empty chair

Is no longer,
Is no longer there

She is now emptiness
She is now air

## 2. ENCHANTMENT

If this were a story
I was telling my sister

A troll from the mountain
Would have stolen her

Or else a twisted magician
Turned her to stone

Or locked her in a tower
Or hidden her deep inside a golden flower

I would have to travel
West of the moon, east of the sun

To find the answer;
I'd speak the charm

And she'd be standing there
Alive and happy, come to no harm

But this is not a story.
Not that kind of story...

### 3. ANGER

Anger is red
The colour of spilled blood

He was all anger,
The man you tried to love

You opened the door
And death was standing there

Red death, red anger
Anger at you

For being so alive
And not destroyed by fear

What do you want? you said.
Red was the answer.

## 4. DREAM

When I sleep you appear
I am a child then
And you are young and still my sister

And it is summer;
I don't know the future,
Not in my dream

I'm going away, you tell me
On a long journey.
I have to go away.

No, stay, I call to you
As you grow smaller:
Stay here with me and play!

But suddenly I'm older
And it's cold and moonless
And it is winter…

## 5. BIRD SOUL

If birds are human souls
What bird are you?
A spring bird with a joyful song?
A high flyer?

Are you an evening bird
Watching the moon
Singing Alone, Alone,
Singing Dead Too Soon?

Are you an owl,
Soft-feathered predator?
Are you hunting, restlessly hunting
The soul of your murderer?

I know you are not a bird,
Though I know you've flown
So far, so far away.
I need you to be somewhere...

## 6. LOST

So many sisters lost
So many lost sisters

Over the years, thousands of years
So many sent away

Too soon into the night
By men who thought they had the right

Rage and hatred
Jealousy and fear

So many sisters killed
Over the years, thousands of years

Killed by fearful men
Who wanted to be taller

Over the years, thousands of years
So many sisters lost

So many tears...

## 7. RAGE

I was too late,
Too late to save you.

I feel the rage and pain
In my own fingers,

In my own hands
I feel the red command

To kill the man who killed you:
That would be only fair:

Him stopped, him nevermore,
In fragments on the floor,

Him shattered.
Why should he still be here

And not you?
Is that what you wish me to do,

Ghost of my sister?
Or would you let him live?

Would you instead forgive?

*CODA:* SONG

If you were a song
What song would you be?

Would you be the voice that sings,
Would you be the music?

When I am singing this song for you
You are not empty air

You are here,
One breath and then another:

You are here with me...

## THE DEAR ONES

But where are they? They can't be nowhere.
It used to be that gypsies took them,
or else the Little People,

who were not little, though enticing.
They were lured into a hill,
those dear ones. There was gold, and dancing.

They should have come home by nine.
You phoned. The clocks chimed
like ice, like metal, heartless.

A week, two weeks: nothing.
Seven years passed. No, a score.
No, a hundred. Make it more.

When they finally reappeared
not a day older
wandering down the road in tatters

in bare feet, their hair all ragged,
those who had waited for them so long
were decades dead.

These were the kinds of stories
we used to tell. They were comforting in a way
because they said

everyone has to be somewhere.
But the dear ones, where are they?
Where? Where? After a while

You sound like a bird.
You stop, but the sorrow goes on calling.
It leaves you and flies out

over the cold night fields,
searching and searching,
over the rivers,
over the emptied air.

## DIGGING UP THE SCYTHIANS

They're digging up the Scythians—
the warrior women, the dagger girls,
the hard riders, tattooed up to the armpits
with sinuous animals, and buried with their weapons—

who were not mythical,
who existed after all
(a bracelet, a trinket, a delicate skull),
laid to rest with honour,
them and their axe-felled horses.

They're digging up the arrow maidens
who wandered cityless, then slept unmelted
in the only houses they ever had:
log rooms, log tombs, deep underground.
Frozen for two thousand years,
them and their embroideries,
their silks and leathers, their feathers,

their hacked arm bones, their broken fingers,
their severed heads.
What did you expect? It was war
and they knew what happened if you lost:
rape, death, death, rape,
as brutal as possible, to set a bad example:
babies and young mothers,
girls and boys, all slaughtered.
That's how it went: straight wipeout.
Which is why they fought.
(And for the loot, if victorious.)

Here they are, the nameless ones,
who are still in some way with us.
They knew what happened.
They know what happens.

# III.

## SEPTEMBER MUSHROOMS

I missed them again this year.
I was immersed elsewhere
when the weather broke
and enough rain came.

In the treeshade, stealthily,
they nosed up through the sandy loam
and the damp leaf litter—

a sliver of colour, then another—
bringing their cryptic news
of what goes on down there:
the slow dissolve of lignum,
the filaments, the little nodes like fists,
assembling their nets and mists.

Some were bright red, some purple,
some brown, some white, some lemon yellow.
Through the night they nudged,
unfurling like moist fans, living sponges,
like radar dishes, listening.

What did they hear in our human world
of so-called light and air?
What word did they send back down
before they withered?
Was it *Beware?*

Look. The remnants:
a leathery globe of dusty spores,
a nibbled pebbly moon,
a dried half-sphere,
a blackened ear.

They arrive every year,
these hollowed-out light-headed ones,
on our doorsteps, our porches,
with their minds full of nothing
but flame, with their vacant stares
that could be glee or menace.

We carved them in our own images:
tricky, but meaning no harm,
not really; or so we say.
Fun at a party
until we get carried away.

Teeth are a feature,
nose holes, eye sockets,
though like us
they aren't skulls yet.

Shine on, orange messengers!
Repel the darkness,
tell Death: No rush.
At least there's some kind of brightness.

Two weeks and the leaves will fall
and you'll be rotting.
Though like the moon you'll return
when your time rolls round again
and again, and again, in the same form.
After we're gone
the work of our knives will survive us.

Smoke gets in my eyes,
my fifteen eyes.
Glass insulation smoulders.
Pink tongues get stuck on it.
Charred cotton candy.

Did I do that?

Palm tree shorn of its head.
Cathedral ceilings, opened up
to the stars, to the stark.
What did they worship in there?
The overhead fans?
The bolsters? The naked bedspread?

I spy.

They cried *O God* to the pillows.
Now ripped and fluttering,
angel feathers.
These hover, slower than me.
See raw finger paint. Red.
Wet still crawling.

Must have missed something.

Better hone in again.
Do some stuttering.
Attapat. Attatat. Attasis. Attaboom.
Accurate this time. Rah.
Anything saved equals failure.

Was I bad?

Teardrops fall and fall.
The rain shower's broken.

The world's burning up. It always did.
Lightning would strike, the resin
in the conifers explode, the black peat smoulder,
greying bones glow slowly, and the fallen leaves
turn brown and writhe, like paper
held to candle. It's the scent of autumn,
oxidation: you can smell it on your skin,
that sunburn perfume.
               Only now
it's burning faster. All those yarns
of charred apocalypse concocted
back when we played with matches—
the ardent histories, the Troyish towers
viewed through toppling smoke, the fine
mirage volcanoes that we mimed
with such delight when setting
marshmallows on fire on purpose,

all those slow-fused epics
packed in anthracite, then buried
under granite mountains, or else thrown
into the deepest sea like djinns
in stoneware bottles—

            All, all are coming true
because we opened the lead seals,
ignored the warning runes,
and let the stories out.
               We had to know.

We had to know
how such tales really end:
and why.

                         They end in flames
because that's what we want:
we want them to.

UPDATE ON WEREWOLVES

In the old days, all werewolves were male.
They burst through their bluejean clothing
as well as their own split skins,
exposed themselves in parks,
howled at the moonshine.
Those things frat boys do.

Went too far with the pigtail-yanking—
growled down into the soft and wriggling
females, who cried *Wee wee*
*wee* all the way to the bone.
Heck, it was only flirting,
plus a canid sense of fun:
See Jane run!

But now it's different:
No longer gender-specific.
Now it's a global threat.

Long-legged women sprint through ravines
in furry warmups, a pack of kinky
models in sado French Vogue getups
and airbrushed short-term memories,
bent on no-penalties rampage.

Look at their red-rimmed paws!
Look at their gnashing eyeballs!
Look at the backlit gauze
of their full-moon subversive halos!
Hairy all over, this belle dame,
and it's not a sweater.

*O freedom, freedom and power!*
they sing as they lope over bridges,
bums to the wind, ripping out throats
on footpaths, pissing off brokers.

Tomorrow they'll be back
in their middle-management black
and Jimmy Choos
with hours they can't account for
and first dates' blood on the stairs.
They'll make a few calls: *Goodbye.*
*It isn't you, it's me. I can't say why.*
At sales meetings,
they'll dream of sprouting tails
right in the audiovisuals.
They'll have addictive hangovers
and ruined nails.

## ZOMBIE

*"Poetry is the past that breaks out in our hearts."*
——RILKE

There you have it: zombie.
Didn't you always suspect?
"Poetry is the past
that breaks out in our hearts"
like a virus, like an infection.
How many poems about
the dead one who isn't dead,
the lost one who semi-persists,
nudging hungrily up
through the plant litter, the waste paper,
scratching against the window?

Take the once-young lover
encountered fifty years later
in the dim light of the foyer.
How blunt and smudged he is!
Mr. Potato Head
without the stick-on features:
someone you grope to remember.
Was it him who licked your neck?

And the clumsy Play-Doh monster
you made at the age of four,
then squashed in a fit of anger
so his colours ran together:
he turns up on your doorstep
on a chill November night,

with the rain whispering *sushi
sushi*, and the tongueless
mouth mumbling your name.

*Stay dead! Stay dead!* you conjure,
you who wanted the past back.
Nothing doing. The creature
ambles through the dim forest,
a red, weeping monosyllable,
a smeared word tasting of sorrow.
Now it mutters and shambles
in a nimbus of dry-ice fog
down the garish overdone corridor
of Gothic clocks, into the mirror.

The hand on your shoulder. The almost-hand:
Poetry, coming to claim you.

# THE ALIENS ARRIVE

*Nine late-night movies*

i.

The aliens arrive.
They are smarter than us, and carnivorous.
You know the rest.

ii.

The aliens arrive
in a mist, in a fine drizzle.
They want to help us,
or so they say.
Then there's a pop, a sizzle.
It was a plot! But why?
A few of us are left alive
after they go away.

iii.

The aliens arrive.
Their leader is a giant head.
It lives in a large glass jar.
It wants to mesmerize us,
though lord knows what for.
Oh wait a minute.
It's a metaphor.

iv.

The aliens arrive.
A white light shines from their pod,
which is shaped like a huge football.
Are they God?

v.

The aliens arrive,
but not in the way you think.
They make their way out through our armpits.
There is screaming, non-stop.
Things get way too pink.

vi.

The aliens arrive
in something that looks like a hubcap.
In fact it is a hubcap,
vintage nineteen fifty-five.
So that's where that thing went!
It wasn't in the garage!
You lied.

vii.

The aliens arrive.
They're ultra-clever octopi
who speak in blots of ink.
They want us to be kind
to one another,
worldwide. First time ever.

Or else. Or else what?
Is this a hopeful sign?
What do you think?


viii.


The aliens arrive.
They've heard about human sex
but don't believe it.
At great risk to themselves
they've come to see.
They send down spies
in the shape of flying eyes
that peek in through our windows.
Oh anthropology!
The horror! The surprise!
What a show!
It almost makes them ill!
What a thrill.
They abduct a hundred humans
through a cosmic straw
and slurp us to another planet
and put us in a zoo.
Unless you have sex on demand
you don't get fed.
They say the equivalent of Ah and Ooo,
also Haha.
Dire, what hunger will do.
It's sex, sex, sex,
every two hours,
alternating with egg sandwiches and beer.
Be careful what you wish for.

ix.

The aliens arrive.
We like the part where we get saved.
We like the part where we get destroyed.
Why do those feel so similar?
Either way, it's an end.
No more just being alive.
No more pretend.

Such curious humans, wondering
what song we sang
to lure so many sailors
to their deaths, granted,

but what sort? Of death,
I mean. Sharp birdclaws
in the groin, a rending pain, fanged
teeth in the neck? Or a last breath
exhaled in bliss, like that
of male praying mantises?

I sit here on my frowsy nest
of neckties, quarterly
reports and jockey shorts
mixed in among the bones and pens,
and fluff my breasts and feathers. Lullaby,

my mini-myths, my hungry egglets,
dreaming in your glowing shells
of our failsafe girly secret.
Mama's right nearby
and Daddy must have loved you:
he gave you all his protein!

Hatching's here. Be strong!
Soon I'll hear a tap-tap-tap, Ahoy!
and out you'll break, my babies,
down-covered, rose-toned, lovely
as a pirouette, a lipstick pout,

a candied violet,
flapping your dainty feathery wings
and ravenous with song.

SPIDER SIGNATURES

Hour by hour I sign myself—
a smear, a dot, a smear,
white semaphore on the black floor.

Spider shit,
what's left of the enticed:
why is it white?
Because my heart is pure,
though I myself am ulterior,

especially under the bookcase:
a fine place for my silken pockets,
my wisps and filaments,
my looms, my precious cradles.

I've always liked books,
by preference paperbacks,
crumbling and flyspecked.
To their texts I add
my annotations, brash and untidy:

moth wings, beetle husks, my own shed skins
like spindly gloves.
Apt simile: I'm mostly fingers.

I don't like the floor, though.
Too visible, I hunch, I scuttle,
a prey to shoes and vacuums,
not to mention whisks.

If you come across me suddenly
you scream: Too many legs,
or is it the eight red eyes,
the glossy blob of abdomen?
Drop of thumb's blood, popped grape:
that's what you'd aim for.

Though it's bad luck to kill me.
Come to terms:
before you were, I am.
I arrange the rain,
I take harsh care

and while you sleep
I hover, the first grandmother.
I trap your nightmares in my net,
eat the seeds of your fears for you,
suck out their ink

and scribble on your windowsill
these minor glosses on *Is, Is, Is,*
white lullabies.

In our language
we have no words for he or she
or him or her.
It helps if you put a skirt or tie
or some such thing
on the first page.

In the case of a rape, it helps also
to know the age:
a child, an elderly?
So we can set the tone.

We also have no future tense:
what will happen is already happening.
But you can add a word like *Tomorrow*
or else *Wednesday*.
We will know what you mean.

These words are for things that can be eaten.
The things that can't be eaten have no words.
Why would you need a name for them?
This applies to plants, birds,
and mushrooms used in curses.

On this side of the table
women do not say No.
There is a word for No, but women do not say it.
It would be too abrupt.
To say No, you can say Perhaps.
You will be understood,
on most occasions.

On that side of the table there are six classes:
unborn, dead, alive,
things you can drink, things you can't drink,
things that cannot be said.

Is it a new word or an old word?
Is it obsolete?
Is it formal or familiar?
How offensive is it? On a scale of one to ten?
Did you make it up?

At the far end of the table
right next to the door,
are those who deal in hazards.
If they translate the wrong word
they might be killed
or at the least imprisoned.
There is no list of such hazards.
They'll find out only after,

when it might not matter to them
about the tie or skirt
or whether they can say No.
In cafés they sit in corners,
backs to the wall.
What will happen is already happening.

IV.

Walking in the madman's wood
over the disquieted dry shushing leaves
in early spring.

The madman loved this wildland
once, before his brain
turned lacework. Must have been
him (when?) who put
this round stone here, topping
the mossy oblong. *Mine.*
And all the tin can
lids and wooden squares,
rough-painted red and nailed to trees
to mark his line:
*mine, mine, mine, mine.*

I shouldn't say that cancelled word:
*madman.* Maybe *lost his mind?*
No, because we don't have minds
as such these days, but tiny snarls
of firefly neural pathways
signalling *no/yes/no*, suspended
in a greyish cloud
inside a round bone bowl.
*Yes:* lovely. *No:* too lonely. *Yes.*
The world that we think we see
is only our best guess.

This must have been his shack,
collapsed now, where he'd—what?

Come sometimes and sit? Hepaticas
wrenched up by sun,
brown tufts of hairbrush grass,
the toppled stove, the wild leeks
so glossy they look wet,
the soft log frilled with mushrooms.

You could get waylaid here, or slip amazed
into your tangled head. You could
just not come back.

# FEATHER

One by handfuls the feathers fell.
Windsheer, sunbleach, owlwar,
some killer with a shotgun,

who can tell?
But I found them here on the quasi-lawn—
I don't know whose torn skin—

calligraphy of wrecked wings,
remains of a god that melted
too near the moon.

A high flyer once,
as we all were.
Every life is a failure

at the last hour,
the hour of dried blood.
But nothing, we like to think,

is wasted, so I picked up one plume from the slaughter,
sharpened and split the quill,
hunted for ink,

and drew this poem
with you, dead bird.
With your spent flight,

with your fading panic,
with your eye spiralling down,
with your night.

## FATAL LIGHT AWARENESS

A thrush crashed into my window:
one lovely voice the less
killed by glass as mirror—

a rich magician's illusion of trees—
and by my laziness:
Why didn't I hang the lattice?

Up there in the night air
among the highrises, music dies
as you fire up your fake sunrises:
your light is the birds' last darkness.

All over everywhere
their feathers are falling—
warm, not like snow—
though melting away to nothing.

We are a dying symphony.
No bird knows this,
but us—we know

what our night magic does.
Our dark light magic.

# FEAR OF BIRDS

You said he was afraid of birds?
How could that be?
Someone so tall?

It wasn't the augury.
Maybe the metal voices,
gold, silver, zinc.

A jingling, a scream, a scrape.
Or a dripping sound in the dry forest.
Tink. Tink. Tink. Tink.
Not to be confused with singing.

Or the close-up craziness of the eyes:
yellow, red, not cozy.
Inside that skull you're not even a thought.

Wings of some sort. Like those of angels,
angels with claws.
Maybe that's it.

A rustling, like thin paper.
Then feathers over the nose and mouth.
Muffled. A white smothering.

You said he was afraid of snow?
Much the same thing.

## SHORT TAKES ON WOLVES

i.

A wolf in pain
admits nothing.
His dinner bit him.
It was a miscalculation,
and now it will be a disaster.

You can't go far with a ripped foot:
among wolves, no doctors.

ii.

A wolf is courteous up to a point.
You have to watch their ears.
Forward, they're willing to listen.
Back, you've bored them.

iii.

Sit in the dark. Keep quiet.
Don't light that cigarette
or smear on the blackfly goo.

It's not a speed-dating venue.
It's not a zoo.
You want to see the wolf
or demand your money back,
but the wolf doesn't want to see you.

iv.

Wolf nightmares involve cars,
long needles, iron muzzles,
cramped cages with hard bars,
creatures who smell like you.

Wolf happy dreams, on the other hand,
are of endless taiga,
dens dug under stones,
limping and stupid caribou,
their tender bones.

# TABLE SETTINGS

Doling out the forks,
little crab claws,
tines filched from lions,

and the knives, incisors
from the tigers we once worshipped,
lacking raw-meat-shearing
tools of our own.

Though our feastfires have faded to candles
we're hooked on the same old gods,
much diminished.

They no longer talk to us
but that's okay:
we do enough talking.

So, Nature. We sit around it,
chew it into rags
with our artful fangs and talons.

Spoons, however:
there are no spoons in Nature,
or not on animals.
We imitate ourselves.

Here, let me help you:
two cupped hands

# IMPROVISATION ON A FIRST LINE BY YEATS

From *Hound Voice*

*Because we love bare hills and stunted trees*
we head north when we can,
past taiga, tundra, rocky shoreline, ice.

Where does it come from, this sparse taste
of ours? How long
did we roam this hardscape, learning by heart
all that we used to know:
turn skin fur side in,
partner with wolves, eat fat, hate waste,
carve spirit, respect the snow,
build and guard flame?

Everything once had a soul,
even this clam, this pebble.
Each had a secret name.
Everything listened.
Everything was real,
but didn't always love you.
You needed to take care.

We long to go back there,
or so we like to feel
when it's not too cold.
We long to pay that much attention.
But we've lost the knack;
also there's other music.
All we hear in the wind's plainsong
is the wind.

## "HEART OF THE ARCTIC"

*Notes from 2017*

bear into rock
rock into bear
bear into rock
depends on how you look

—

A white rock on the hillside
becomes a bear
flings out fangs and fur
when you aren't looking

that's how things move around.

Before you know it you've turned to stone
because a stone ate you.

Though it broke its tusks on your heart
your heart of a heron
that's harder and has more teeth
than anything here.

—

In a sunken angle of crashed rock chunks carved off from the
        mountain
down there where a stream edges through,
two creatures on the orange-green moss:

a purple flower, a River Beauty
nobody else will see
except this one bee,

and a cigarette butt.

A careless person has been here.
Nothing cares.

—

Quick flicker of lemming.
Match flare in the sedge.
It doesn't know it is fire.
Gone   here   gone
from the eye's corner.

—

You drift among these giant rocks
like a ghost   a wind   a ghost
like a lost plastic bag
roaming these moors for thirty years.
Like a membrane.

To the waterfalls to the wrinkled hills to the pebbles
you are translucent.

In the shore water there's a jellyfish
blush-coloured and dead,
already dissolving.

My darlings, who have chosen
your outdoor gear with such care—
everything matching—
you are like that.


—


Many have heard voices
they thought were the voices of gods
or just one god
telling them what to do

or a chunk of stone
that says it wants to be a statue

or an animal
that offers up its life to you,
tells you to kill it.


—


Where is the voice coming from?
Why can only some hear it?

What was that bird I heard chirping
that was not the river that was not my own creaky backpack
that was not in my head?

What bird? Where? I'm listening, he said.

But there's nothing.

# PLASTICENE SUITE

### I. ROCK-LIKE OBJECT ON BEACH

The Paleocene the Eocene
the Miocene the Pleistocene
and now we're here: the Plasticene.

Look, a rock made of sand
and one of lime, and one of quartz,
and one of what is this?

It's black and striped and slippery,
not exactly rock
and not not.

On the beach at any rate.
Petrified oil, with a vein of scarlet,
part of a bucket maybe.

When we're gone and the aliens come
to puzzle out our fossils:
will this be evidence?

Of us: of our too-brief history,
our cleverness, our thoughtlessness,
our sudden death?

You could turn it into oil
by cooking it: this has been done.
First you'd have to collect it.
Also there would be a smell.

Some supermarkets have banned it.
Also drinking straws.
Maybe there will be a tax
or other laws.

There are microbes that eat it—
they've been discovered.
But the temperature has to be high:
no good in the north sea.

You can press it into fake lumber
but only some kinds.
And building blocks, ditto.

You can scoop it out of rivers
before it gets to the sea.
But then what? What do you do with it?

With the overwhelming ongoing
never-ending outpouring?

## 3. FOLIAGE

*"a scrap of black plastic—the defining foliage of the oil age"*
MARK COCKER, *OUR PLACE*


It sprouts everywhere, this foliage.
Up in the trees, like mistletoe,
or caught in the marshes

or blooming in the ponds like waterlilies,
gaudy and frilly,
rippling as if alive

or washing onto the beaches, neo-seaweed
of torn bags, cast wrappers, tangled rope
shredded by tides and rocks.

But unlike true foliage it's rootless
and gives nothing back,
not even one empty calorie.

Who plants it, this useless crop?
Who harvests it?
Who can say Stop?

Inside the barebones
ribs it's all bright colour:
a tag a ribbon
a failed balloon
a strip of silver foil
a spring a wheel a coil

What should have been there
inside the sad bag
of wispy feathers
inside the dead bird child?

It should have been the fuel
for wings, it should have been
upsoaring over a clean sea;
not this glittering mess,
this festering nestwork

## 5. EDITORIAL NOTES

One note might be (she said)
to pull back somewhat
from exhortation and despair

Instead (she said)
try to provide
an experiential under

understanding of human
human (she said) impact
human pact

then let people
let people come
let people come to their own

conclusions.
Own their conclusions.
She said:

There is some danger in this.

## 6. SORCERER'S APPRENTICE

You know the old tale:
a machine made by the Devil
that grinds out anything you wish for
with a magic word

and some idiot wishes for salt,
and out comes the salt, more and more,
but he failed to get a handle
on the charm to turn it off

so he throws the thing into the sea,
and that's why the sea is salt.

The Sorcerer's Apprentice—
it's the same story: *Go* is easy,
*Stop* is the hard part.
In the beginning no one thinks about it.
Then *Wait* is too late.

In our case the sorcerer is dead,
whoever he was to begin with
and we've lost the instructions

and the magic machine grinds on and on
spewing out mountains of whatnot
and we throw it all into the sea
as we have always done
and this will not end well

## 7. WHALES

Everyone cried when they saw it
in the square blue sea of the TV:
so big and sad

a mother whale
carrying her child
for three days, mourning
its death from toxic plastic.

So big and sad
we can hardly grasp it:
how did we do this by just living
in the normal way,

manoeuvring our way through
package and wrapping,
cutting our way to our food
through the layer by layer that
keeps it fresher,
and doesn't everyone?

What happened before?
How did we ever survive
with only paper and glass and tin
and hemp and leather and oilskin?

But now there's a dead whale
right there on the screen:

so big and sad
something must be done.

It will be! Will it be?
Will we decide to, finally?

## 8. LITTLE ROBOT

This is the little robot
they have just invented
with its cute dollface of soft plastic.
Its expression is confiding
though slightly fearful:
it's designed to learn like a child.

We give it objects:
it fingers them, explores,
it bites and questions,
it plays with them, absorbs.
Then it gets bored
and drops things on the floor.

There might be breakage,
maybe even whimpering.
Does it care?
Have we really gone that far?

It's learning like a child:
how to predict—they tell us—
likely future events:
This will cause that.

Little dollface robot,
what will you make of yourself
in this world we are making?
What will you make of us?

Where will you bestow yourself
when you are obsolete?
On what cosmic trashheap?
Or will you live forever?
Will we become your ancestors,
rapacious and tedious?
Or will you erase us?
Will you drop us on the floor?
Would that be better?

## 9. THE BRIGHT SIDE

But look on the bright side,
you say.
Has there ever been such brightness?

Has there ever been a flower as bright
that has lasted as long as this?
In winter snow, after a funeral?

Has there ever been a red as red,
a blue as blue?
And so inexpensive too!

Has there ever been a bucket
as light as this, to carry water
into the villages?

Why should we use the heavy one
so easily broken?
Not to mention the orange canoe.

As for your voice, two thousand miles away
but as clear as whistling, right in my ear—
how else could it get here?

Don't tell me this is not beautiful—
as beautiful as the day!
Or some days.

(And the beloved twistable
pea-green always dependable
ice-cube tray ...)

A mist of thin fat yellows the air.
We breathe hot pudding.
The leaves in the garden are crisp,
like antique taffeta. The former garden.
A touch and they shatter.
Forget the lawn—
the former lawn—
though the dandelions prosper:
they've outlasted our flimsy hybrids.
Their roots grip baked clay.

All day it's been pending, the rain.
It gathers, it withholds.
We thumb our touchscreens,
consulting the odds
on the radar maps: green puddles flow
from west to east,
vanishing before they hit
the dot that's us.
A stretched red dot, like a comic-book voice
devoid of words,
like an upside-down teardrop.

That's where we're living now,
inside this dot
the colour of a heated toaster;
inside this dry red bubble.

We stand on the non-lawn,
arms outstretched, mouths open.

Will it be burn or drown?
Though we've forgotten the incantation,
the chant, the dance,
we invoke a vertical ocean,
pure blue, pure water.
*Let it come down.*

Oh children, will you grow up in a world without birds?
Will there be crickets, where you are?
Will there be asters?
Clams, at a minimum.
Maybe not clams.

We know there will be waves.
Not much life needed for those.
A breeze, a storm, a cyclone.
Ripples, as well. Stones.
Stones are consoling.

There will be sunsets, as long as there is dust.
There will be dust.

Oh children, will you grow up in a world without songs?
Without pines, without mosses?

Will you spend your life in a cave,
a sealed cave with an oxygen line,
until there's a power failure?
Will your eyes blank out like the eggwhite eyes
of sunless fish?
In there, what will you wish for?

Oh children, will you grow up in a world without ice?
Without mice, without lichens?

Oh children, will you grow up?

Pale mauve, pale rose, pale blue,
quirks of the atmosphere:
a bleached Easter.
We gods preside at our own altar.
Hawk face of an old man,
a crone's tyrant jowls.
Lots of jewels.
Offside, lone fisherman in a metal boat
flings away shark parts:
a flurry of beaks and wings.

Lunchtime. Peristalsis of the heart.
Blood squeezed through.
Grit from a lost glacier sifts into our gullets—
grey sand ground from granite—
also limestone: small teeth, fine spines
and midget shells.
They harden us. We open bottles.

Do we have goodwill?
To all mankind?
Not any more.
Did we ever?

When the gods frown, the weather's bad.
When they smile the sun shines.
We smile all the time now,
smiles of the lobotomized,
and the world fries.

Sorry about that. We got stupid.
We drink martinis and go on cruises.
Whatever we touch turns red.

We pick our way over the slippery rocks
over the stream's foam feathers,
gingerly, in the mist, in the light rain.
Such colours here: crowberries,
round black eyes among the leaves,
red, plum, pink, and orange,
though in a week they'll vanish,
a fact not lost on us.
What's here? A mound of fine white hair?
Has someone been buried?
Yes, many, over the years,
though this is only lichen.

Here are the ravens, as if on cue.
Will you be next? they ask us.
They understand waned flesh:
so eager for a beakful.
Wait a little, we say to them.
Everything in good time.
Meanwhile the ponds are beautiful,
the yellow stones, green moss, the scurvy grass,
the long-abandoned graves, the small old willows.

V.

# ONE DAY

*(The Three Fates sing backup)*


One day I will be old,
you said; let's say
while hanging up the wash—
the sheets, the pillowcases—
with their white smell of June rain
in the years when you still did that
and pear blossoms fell around you
joyous as weddings
and your brain sang Yeah yeah yeah
like a backup group,
three girls with long legs
and thigh-high boots, wagging their miniskirts
like bees announcing honey in some complex dance
in time.

In time my eyes will shrink, Yeah yeah
my mouth will fill with metal,
my spine will crumble, Yeah yeah
yeah, sang the three lithe girls
who now had silver makeup
and green spiked hair.
But maybe I'll get wisdom,
you said, laughing,
like stepping through a door.
Oh yeah! they sang. Fuck that!
Who needs it anyway?

Then you forgot them.

Today you're poking with your stick
among the wilted hostas
in the quiet garden.
Where is it? you say
to the last blue asters,
to the yellow leaves floating in the pool
of the round stone birdbath.
Where is that wisdom?
Not to mention the music.
It must be around here somewhere.
Now that I need it.

Nobody sings backup now.
Now they just whisper
in their pale yellow camouflage.
They've got sticks too.
Over there, they say, oh yeah.
The wisdom.
Try the geraniums.

You pry with your stick:
Just earth and roots. A stone.
Maybe it's a door, you say.
Yeah, yeah, they whisper.
But nothing's locked. There's nothing
to it. Never was.
Just open.
Just walk down.

The pen reft of the hand,
the knife ditto.
The cello reft of the bow.
The word reft of the speaker
and vice versa.

The word *reft:*
who says that any more?
Yet it was honed, like all words,
in the mouths of hundreds, of thousands,
rolled like a soundstone over and over,
sharpened by the now dead
until it reached this form:
*reft*
*reft*
a cloth ripped asunder.
*Asunder*—minor sunset,
peach clouds faded to slate:
another loss.

And what to do with these binoculars,
sixty years old or more,
reft of their war?

How quickly we're skimming through time,
leaving behind us
a trail of muffin crumbs
and wet towels and hotel soaps
like white stones in the forest.
But something's eroded them:
we can't trace them back
to that meadow where we began so eagerly
with the berry-filled cups, and the parents
who had not yet abandoned us
to take their chances in the ground.

Our tropical clothing's remorseless:
it fully intends to outlast us.
We're shrivelling inside it,
leaking calcium from our bones.
Then there's our crafty hats:
we catch them sneering in mirrors.
We could afford new T-shirts,
daring ones, with rude slogans,
but it seems a waste:
we've got too many already.
Also they'd gang up on us,
they'd creep around on the floor,
they'd tangle our ankles,
then we'd fall down the stairs.

Despite all this we're travelling fast,
we're travelling faster than light.
It's almost next year,

it's almost last year,
it's almost the year before:
familiar, but we can't swear to it.
What about this outdoor bar,
the one with the stained-glass palm tree?
We know we've been here already.
Or were we? Will we ever be?
Will we ever be again?
Is it far?

My truelove limps along the street
hayfoot   strawfoot   lame foot
who once was an army marcher.

He's up there now, ahead, in silhouette
against bright windows, against
the leather coats, the Sunglass Hut,
the Ladies' Jewellery:

Hayfoot, straw...
Now gone. Blended with shadow.

Maybe not himself. Not the same one,
the strider in the autumn woods, leaves yellow,
a whiff of snow
on the frozen ground, bears around,
a skim of ice on the ponds.
then uphill, hayfoot, me gasping
to keep up.

What happened? What became?
Why are you still walking?
said the doctor. You have no knee.
Yet on he limps, unseen by me
behind the corner,
willing himself to get there:
to some warm haven, kindly nook
or drink, or chair.

The red light changes. Darkness clots:
it's him all right,
not even late, his cane foot
hayfoot, straw,
slow march. It's once

it's once upon
a time, it's cane
as tic, as tock.

## MR. LIONHEART

Mr. Lionheart is away today.
He comes and goes,
he flickers on and off.
You might have heard a roar,
you might not.

What is it he forgot
this last time?
I don't mean the keys, the hat.
I mean his tawny days,
the sun, the golden running.
All of our furry dancing.
It returns to him in flashes,

but then what? Then regret
because we're not.
There's birdsong, however,
from birds whose names have vanished.

Birds don't need them, those lost names.
We needed them, but that was then.
Now, who cares?
Lions don't know they are lions.
They don't know how brave they are.

# INVISIBLE MAN

It was a problem in comic books:
drawing an invisible man.
They'd solve it with a dotted line
that no one but us could see,

us with our snub noses pressed to the paper,
the invisible glass between us and the place
where invisible men can exist.

That's who is waiting for me:
an invisible man
defined by a dotted line:

the shape of an absence
in your place at the table,
sitting across from me,
eating toast and eggs as usual
or walking ahead up the drive,
a rustling of the fallen leaves,
a slight thickening of the air.

It's you in the future,
we both know that.
You'll be here but not here,
a muscle memory, like hanging a hat
on a hook that's not there any longer.

No dancing any more, but still
wearing my silver shoes

my silver slippers,
all of their wishes used up

and no way to get home.
I'll skip dinner, the kind with linens

and candles lit for two. I'll be alone,
sitting across from an absence.

Oh where did you go, and when?
It wasn't to Kansas.

I'll perch in this hotel room solo
and nibble a square of cheddar

saved up from the plane.
Also the salted almonds.

These will tide me over.
I won't be hungry.

I'll act as if I am busy.
But none of this will defend me:

not the silken bedsheets
the pillows ballooning aloft,

not even the happiness travel mag
with its conjuror's dreams—

the winged monkey brain
flying me to neverland,

such coziness and shelter—
those don't make up for it.

*It*, the moment we know is coming,
the click of the seconds

on the skyblue bedside alarm,
countdown as the flying house descends

to silent crash, dead witchy heart
plus empty silver shoes, end stop.

Outside we see a shrivelling,
but from within, as felt
by heart and breath and inner skin, how different,
how vast   how calm   how part of everything
how starry dark. Last breath. Divine
perhaps. Perhaps relief. The lovers caught
and sealed inside a cavern,
voices raised in one last hovering
duet, until the small wax light
goes out. Well anyway
I held your hand and maybe
you held mine
as the stone or universe closed in
around you.
Though not me. I'm still outside.

# FLATLINE

Things wear out. Also fingers.
Gnarling sets in.
Your hands crouch in their mittens,
forget chopsticks, and buttons.

Feet have their own agendas.
They scorn your taste in shoes
and ignore your trails, your maps.

Ears are superfluous:
What are they for,
those alien pink flaps?
Skull fungus.

The body, once your accomplice,
is now your trap.
The sunrise makes you wince:
too bright, too flamingo.

After a lifetime of tangling,
of knotted snares and lacework,
of purple headspace tornadoes
with their heartrace and rubble,
you crave the end of mazes

and pray for a white shore,
an ocean with its horizon;
not—so much—bliss,
but a flat line you steer for.

No more hiss and slosh,
no reefs, no deeps,
no throat rattle of gravel.

It sounds like this:

# DISENCHANTED CORPSE

*Disenchanted corpse—*
this seems to be the new name
for a dead body.

The magic's left you:
that flicker, that sparkle, gone.
Dried firefly.

But if you're now disenchanted,
who enchanted you, back then?
What magus or sorceress cast over you
the net of words, the charm?
Placed the scroll in your golem's
mouth of mud?

*Life, life,* you sang
with every cell,
compelled into dancing
as the spell held you enchained
and you burned air.
Then it was midnight, and a pale flame rose
from you, and you collapsed into bone.

Disenchanted corpse, they say.
Inert. Emptied of prayer,
limp to all conjures.
A figment, a fragment.
Lifeless. Less.

Or are you? Or is it?

# DEARLY

It's an old word, fading now.
Dearly did I wish.
Dearly did I long for.
I loved him dearly.

I make my way along the sidewalk
mindfully, because of my wrecked knees
about which I give less of a shit
than you may imagine
since there are other things, more important—
wait for it, you'll see—

bearing half a coffee
in a paper cup with—
dearly do I regret it—
a plastic lid—
trying to remember what words once meant.

Dearly.
How was it used?
Dearly beloved.
Dearly beloved, we are gathered.
Dearly beloved, we are gathered here
in this forgotten photo album
I came across recently.

Fading now,
the sepias, the black and whites, the colour prints,
everyone so much younger.
The Polaroids.

What is a Polaroid? asks the newborn.
Newborn a decade ago.

How to explain?
You took the picture and then it came out the top.
The top of what?
It's that baffled look I see a lot.
So hard to describe
the smallest details of how—
all these dearly gathered together—
of how we used to live.
We wrapped up garbage
in newspaper tied with string.
What is newspaper?
You see what I mean.

String though, we still have string.
It links things together.
A string of pearls.
That's what they would say.
How to keep track of the days?
Each one shining, each one alone,
each one then gone.
I've kept some of them in a drawer on paper,
those days, fading now.
Beads can be used for counting.
As in rosaries.
But I don't like stones around my neck.

Along this street there are many flowers,
fading now because it is August
and dusty, and heading into fall.
Soon the chrysanthemums will bloom,

flowers of the dead, in France.
Don't think this is morbid.
It's just reality.

So hard to describe the smallest details of flowers.
This is a stamen, nothing to do with men.
This is a pistil, nothing to do with guns.
It's the smallest details that foil translators
and myself too, trying to describe.
See what I mean.
You can wander away. You can get lost.
Words can do that.

Dearly beloved, gathered here together
in this closed drawer,
fading now, I miss you.
I miss the missing, those who left earlier.
I miss even those who are still here.
I miss you all dearly.
Dearly do I sorrow for you.

*Sorrow:* that's another word
you don't hear much any more.
I sorrow dearly.

## BLACKBERRIES

In the early morning an old woman
is picking blackberries in the shade.
It will be too hot later
but right now there's dew.

Some berries fall: those are for squirrels.
Some are unripe, reserved for bears.
Some go into the metal bowl.
Those are for you, so you may taste them
just for a moment.
That's good times: one little sweetness
after another, then quickly gone.

Once, this old woman
I'm conjuring up for you
would have been my grandmother.
Today it's me.
Years from now it might be you,
if you're quite lucky.

The hands reaching in
among the leaves and spines
were once my mother's.
I've passed them on.
Decades ahead, you'll study your own
temporary hands, and you'll remember.
Don't cry, this is what happens.

Look! The steel bowl
is almost full. Enough for all of us.

The blackberries gleam like glass,
like the glass ornaments
we hang on trees in December
to remind ourselves to be grateful for snow.

Some berries occur in sun,
but they are smaller.
It's as I always told you:
the best ones grow in shadow.

# ACKNOWLEDGEMENTS

Some of these poems have previously appeared in the following periodicals:

*Audubon*
*Harper's Bazaar*
*The New Yorker*
*Poetry Ireland Review*

and the online platform Wattpad

and in the following anthologies:

*Anthropocene*, Edward Burtynsky with Jennifer Baichwal and Nicholas de Pencier (Göttingen: Steidl, 2018).

*The Best American Poetry 2019*, eds. David Lehman and Major Jackson (New York: Scribner, 2019).

*Bringing Back the Birds: Exploring Migration and Preserving Birdscapes throughout the Americas*, American Bird Conservancy (Seattle: Braided River, 2019).

*Cutting Edge: New Stories of Mystery and Crime by Women Writers*, ed. Joyce Carol Oates (New York: Akashic Books, 2019).

*Fifty Shades of Feminism*, eds. Lisa Appignanesi, Rachel Holmes, and Susie Orbach (London: Virago, 2013).

*Freeman's: Power*, ed. John Freeman (New York: Grove Press, 2018).

*Kwe: Standing With Our Sisters*, ed. Joseph Boyden (Toronto: Penguin Canada, 2014).

*Tales of Two Planets: Stories of Climate Change and Inequality in a Divided World*, ed. John Freeman (New York: Penguin Books, 2020).

The poems "Oh Children" and "Blackberries" were previously recorded on vinyl record as part of the *7-inches for Planned Parenthood* album box set.

"Songs for Murdered Sisters" is a song cycle written for baritone Joshua Hopkins, in honour of his own murdered sister. The music was composed by Jake Heggie.